GUINNESS W★RLD RECORDS™

GUINNESS WORLD RECORDS™

BIGGEST, TALLEST, GREATEST!

Records of Overwhelming Size

Collect and Compare with

FEARLESS FEATS:
Incredible Records of Human Achievement

WILD LIVES:
Outrageous Animal & Nature Records

JUST OUTRAGEOUS!:
Extraordinary Records of Unusual Facts & Feats

DEADLY DISASTERS:
Catastrophic Records in History

MYSTERIES & MARVELS OF THE PAST:
Historical Records of Phenomenal Discoveries

GUINNESS WORLD RECORDS

BIGGEST, TALLEST, GREATEST!

Records of Overwhelming Size

Compiled by Kris Hirschmann & Ryan Herndon

For Guinness World Records:
Laura Barrett Plunkett, Craig Glenday,
Stuart Claxton, Michael Whitty, and Laura Jackson

SCHOLASTIC INC.
New York   Toronto   London   Auckland   Sydney
Mexico City   New Delhi   Hong Kong   Buenos Aires

Guinness World Records Limited has a very thorough accreditation system for records verification. However, while every effort is made to ensure accuracy, Guinness World Records Limited cannot be held responsible for any errors contained in this work. Feedback from our readers on any point of accuracy is always welcomed.

© 2007 Guinness World Records Limited, a HIT Entertainment Limited Company.

ISBN-13: 978-0-439-89829-4
ISBN-10: 0-439-89829-3

Designed by Michelle Martinez Design, Inc.
Photo Research by Els Rijper, Sarah Parrish
Records from the Archives of Guinness World Records

12 11 10 9 8 7 6 5 4 3 2 1   7 8 9 10 11/0

Printed in the U.S.A.

First printing, February 2007

Visit Guinness World Records at www.guinnessworldrecords.com

Contents

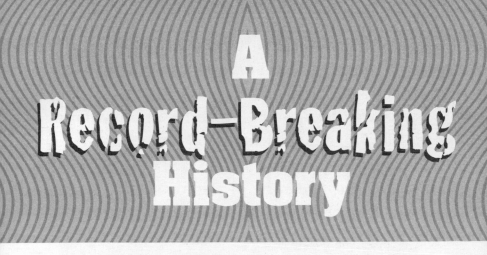

A Record-Breaking History

The idea for Guinness World Records grew out of a question. In 1951, Sir Hugh Beaver, the managing director of the Guinness Brewery, wanted to know which was the fastest game bird in Europe — the golden plover or the grouse? Some people argued that it was the grouse. Others claimed it was the plover. A book to settle the debate did not exist until Sir Hugh discovered the knowledgeable twin brothers Norris and Ross McWhirter, who lived in London.

Like their father and grandfather, the McWhirter twins loved information. They were kids when they started clipping interesting facts from newspapers and memorizing important dates in world history. As well as learning the names of every river, mountain range, and nation's capital, they knew the record for pole squatting (196 days in 1954), which language had only one irregular verb (Turkish), and that the grouse — flying at a timed speed of 43.5 miles per hour — is faster than the golden plover at 40.4 miles per hour.

Norris and Ross served in the Royal Navy during World War II, graduated from college, and launched their own fact-finding business called McWhirter Twins, Ltd. They were the perfect people to compile the book of records that Sir Hugh Beaver searched for yet could not find.

The first edition of *The Guinness Book of Records* was published on August 27, 1955, and since then has been published in 37 languages and more than 100 countries. In 2000, the book title changed to *Guinness World Records* and has set an incredible record of its own: Excluding non-copyrighted books such as the Bible and the Koran, *Guinness World Records* is the best-selling book of all time!

Today, the official Keeper of the Records keeps a careful eye on each Guinness World Record, compiling and verifying the greatest the world has to offer — from the fastest and the tallest to the slowest and the smallest, with everything in between.

Introduction

How
Large Is That?

For more than 50 years, Guinness World Records has verified the facts and stories behind the larger-than-life record-breakers. In this collection, we focus on prodigious people, plants, animals, and tons of super-size stuff.

Go 10 rounds with the heaviest twins, slip into an elephant-size suit of armor, giggle and jiggle at the sight of mosaics made from Jell-O and toast, and take a bath with more than 2,000 rubber duckies — these are just a few of the biggest record-holders in the world!

"*How* large is that?" We'll give you the exact stats of the tallest to the heaviest, the longest to the largest, in craters, cars, and collections!

Chapter 1
Prodigious People

Sometimes humans can't help going to extremes, and the prodigious people you'll meet on the next few pages prove it. Tower over the crowd with the tallest people alive today, play giraffe with the long-necked members of Myanmar's Paduang tribe, and go belly to belly with the beefiest twins. You can gawk at a hair-raising accessory that was once considered the height of fashion. Stand tall and get ready to live large!

A Giant Condition

Some extremely tall people have a condition known as **pituitary gigantism**. The pituitary gland is a pea-size organ that controls the body's growth. If this gland makes too much growth hormone during childhood, a person grows faster than normal. The term "giant" refers to people who are between 7 to 8 feet tall, and suffer from an over-active pituitary gland. (The term does not apply to basketball players and others who are big due to genetics.) Sandy Allen (see Record 2) was 6 feet tall by the time she was 10 years old! She had to have an operation to remove the out-of-control parts of her pituitary gland when she was a teenager or she would have eventually died from her condition.

Tallest Living Man

It sounds like a tall tale — but it's true, and the **Tallest Living Man** has the medical records to prove it. As a child and young teen, Xi Shun of China stood eye to eye with his peers. But around the age of 16, Xi started to shoot upward. He grew and grew for seven years, eventually topping out at a height of 7 feet 8.95 inches. On January 15, 2005, Xi showed no signs of any conditions that cause abnormal growth during his measurement and examination at Chifeng City Hospital in Inner Mongolia, China. In short, he's a medical mystery *and* a Guinness World Record-holder. See Xi Shun in full color on the front cover of this book. You can't miss him — he's the tallest of the group!

Tallest Living Woman

Step right up and look Sandy Allen straight in the eyes — but you might need a boost! Standing an amazing 7 feet 7.25 inches tall and weighing in at 314 pounds, this resident of Shelbyville, Indiana, USA, has been the **Tallest Living Woman** since 1976 (pictured). Sandy towers above regular folks and even edges out the loftiest professional basketball players. Sandy doesn't play b-ball herself, but she does have something in common with the stars of the NBA: super-size shoes. In fact, Sandy wears secondhand size-22 sneakers donated by Indiana Pacers basketball player Rick "The Dunking Dutchman" Smits. Those are some big shoes to fill, but this lady manages the "feet" with no trouble at all!

Heaviest Twins

No, you're not see-ing double. You're look-ing at the **Heaviest Twins**, Billy Leon and Benny Lloyd McCrary, who were born in 1946 in Hendersonville, North Carolina (pictured). The McCrary brothers were normal in size until age 6, when severe cases of the measles damaged their pituitary glands. Immediately afterward, both boys started to bulk up. By November 1978, Billy and Benny weighed 742 pounds and 723 pounds, respectively, with waists measuring 84 inches each. Billy died after a motorcycle acci-dent in 1979, while Benny succumbed to heart fail-ure in 2001.

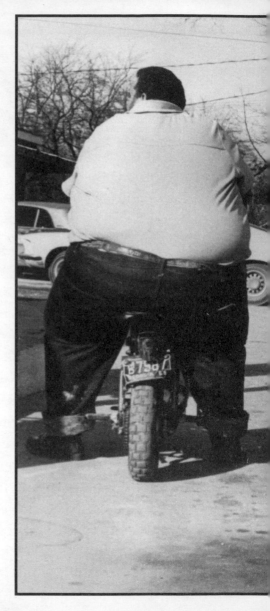

Living Large

Billy and Benny McCrary were celebrities during their lifetimes. Known professionally as the McGuire brothers, the portly pair made a living wrestling, doing daredevil motorcycle stunts, and even telling jokes on a Las Vegas stage.

They got their start at a local fair, when a photographer from *Life* magazine snapped the now-famous photo of the massive men riding teeny-tiny minibikes (left). The picture caught the public's attention and brought the McCrary twins to the attention of Guinness World Records. "They told us they saw us in *Life* magazine and wanted to put us in [their] book. We said, 'Sure!' That was in '68, and we've been in it ever since," laughed Benny in one interview.

Highest Hairstyle

To understand the meaning of the phrase "big hair," you'll need to flip your calendar back to the mid-1700s. Around this time, Queen Marie Antoinette of France was amusing herself by wearing increasingly large and elaborate headpieces to royal balls (see illustration). Just how large were these headpieces? In 1775, Marie Antoinette sported a wig that was said to be 36 inches tall, making it the **Highest Hairstyle** in history. The way-high wig was decorated with a mass of ribbons and feathers that made it even taller and heavier. The humongous hairpiece was the height of fashion at the time, but it was undoubtedly a real pain in the neck to wear!

Longest Necks

Strong necks and high fashion are plentiful among the women of Myanmar's Padaung or Kareni tribal groups. Around age 5 or 6, girls from these tribes start wearing copper coils around their necks. Extra twists are added over time. The heavy coil slowly compresses the wearer's rib cage and collarbones, creating a slender, giraffe-like neck that the tribal society considers the height of feminine beauty (pictured). The **Longest Neck** known to have been shaped using this method was 15.75 inches. That's more than double the height of this book! It's an odd effect from a Western perspective. But as with any cosmetic procedure, beauty is in the eye — or in this case, the neck — of the beholder.

Stretching the Truth?

Some sources claim that the stretched necks of Padaung and Kareni women weaken to such a severe degree that, were the coils removed, these women's necks could not support their heads. Therefore, these tribal women must always wear their neck decorations once the stretching process begins at the age of 5. However, other sources claim the women are in no such danger. They can, and often do, remove the coils for cleaning. "This does not cause their necks to collapse," explains one Thai travel guide. Which version is true? Maybe it depends on the length of the neck!

Chapter 2
Weighty Wildlife

Mother Nature sure knows how to grow them — and it seems that she was in a generous mood with these colossal critters. Toads as large as human babies, birds the size of cars, sharks with enormous built-in whips, and hippos with drive-in mouths are all on display in the next few pages. For a slight change of pace, you'll also read about an outfit created to protect one of the most ponderous pachyderms!

Largest Toad

It's going to take you a long time to count the warts on Prinsen, the **Largest Toad** ever discovered (not pictured). Owned by Håkan Forsberg of Sweden, this astonishing amphibian weighed 5 pounds 13.5 ounces and measured 15 inches from snout to vent in March 1991. How could Prinsen be so huge? Good nutrition is always part of the formula, but as a cane or marine toad (*Bufo marinus*), Prinsen was born with large growth genes. Native to tropical South America, adults of this species average about 1 pound in weight, and 4 to 6 inches in length (pictured). That's a whole lotta toad, but as Håkan and other amphibian admirers would say, the extra bulk is just more to love.

Hopping Continents

With their big bodies, it's not surprising that cane toads are big eaters. These chunky critters will gobble down anything they can fit in their mouths, including bugs, birds, lizards, mice, snakes, plants, and garbage. Because of this habit, cane toads have been collected and sold to farmers around the world. The toads are released in crop fields, where they are supposed to act as living pest-control devices.

At one time, cane toads were found only in South America. Today, because of farm use, these amphibians poplate Australia, Florida, Papua New Guinea, the Philippines, Japan, and others. In most cases, the toads are not controlling the pests but have *become* pests. It just goes to show that people can't predict what will happen when they ignore an old but sensible saying: "Don't mess with Mother Nature!"

Largest Wingspan of Any Living Species of Bird

The wandering albatross (*Diomedea exulans*) isn't the biggest bird by weight, but we defy you not to duck if one comes swooping your way. Boasting the **Largest Wingspan of Any Living Species of Bird**, these amazing aviators often measure 10 to 11 feet from wing tip to wing tip (pictured). One record-setting male specimen, caught by members of the Antarctic research ship USNS *Eltanin* in the Tasman Sea on September 18, 1965, had a wingspan of 11 feet 11 inches — the length of a Mini Cooper automobile! The wandering albatross is a naturally gifted glider, able to coast across Earth's southern oceans for weeks at a time without landing. How do young albatrosses learn this skill? They just wing it!

Longest Fin

It's common sense to avoid a shark's mouth. But in the case of the long-tailed thresher shark (*Alopias vulpinus*), you have to watch out for the other end (pictured). Found worldwide in temperate and tropical seas, these scary swimmers have huge scythe-shaped *caudal* (tail) fins that account for about half the length of their bodies. In other words, a 20-foot shark may sport a 10-foot upper tail lobe — the **Longest Fin** of any fish in the sea. A thresher shark uses its astonishing appendage as a built-in weapon, whipping it through the water to strike and stun prey. The fin's hungry owner can then gulp down the injured animals without any trouble.

RECORD 9

Cute Not Cuddly

Do you think hippos are cute? Their black, button-size eyes look like teddy bear peepers, and their tubby tummies seem to say, "Squeeze me!" In reality, hippos can be fierce, bad-tempered mammals that will fight to defend their territories. A squabble between two hippos is no big deal, because the fighters are evenly matched. But it's a different story when a human wanders too close to a hippo's home. An adult male human weighs about 180 pounds, while an adult male hippo weighs up to 7,000 pounds. Between their weight —— and teeth the size of baseball bats —— hippos are the deadliest mammals in Africa, killing more people each year than lions, crocodiles, cape buffaloes, or any of the continent's other powerful predators!

Largest Mouth for a Land Animal

Open wide and say "Ahhh!" You're staring into the gullet of the African hippopotamus (*Hippopotamus amphibious*), which can open its jaws to almost 180 degrees. In a full-grown male, this works out to a gape of about 4 feet, which is the **Largest Mouth for a Land Animal**. A human child could stand upright inside a hippo's mouth with no trouble — space-wise, at least. The kid *might* have a problem with the hippo's huge, sharp canine teeth, which measure anywhere from 28 to 48 inches each. Why such terrifying teeth on a plant eater? Maybe Mother Nature thought the hippo needed something impressive to carry around in that majestic maw (pictured in the special color insert).

Largest Suit of Animal Armor

What's a poor war elephant to do when enemy arrows start to fly? Suit up! The **Largest Suit of Animal Armor** was made between the late sixteenth and early seventeenth century in northern India during the Mughul Empire (pictured). Designed to fit an adult male Asian elephant, the original outfit used 8,439 metal plates and weighed 350 pounds. Today, the gigantic garment is missing a few panels, but it still tips the scales at 260 pounds. Even that reduced weight seems like a backbreaking burden, but a war elephant could easily lift the load along with several soldiers and their weapons. With this kind of strength, it's no wonder these massive mammals were once considered the ultimate battle accessories.

Chapter 3
Gigantic Greenery

Overgrown . . . and overwhelming! That's the unifying theme behind these five entries, which look at some of the most majestic plants and greenery feats. Get a seal's-eye view of an underwater forest, stroll for hours between the tree-size shoots of the most massive plant known to science, and . . . HEY! Did that tree just fling a bowling ball at you? Read about this fauna, which really know how to grow for a record!

An Underwater Lawn

Did you know that seaweed is an ingredient in some of our favorite foods? Pacific giant kelp contains a gummy substance called alginate that is used to smooth and thicken ice cream, sauces, canned goods, salad dressings, and several other food products. Special harvesting boats with underwater blades steam slowly above a kelp forest, slicing through the tops of the fronds and pulling them out of the water on giant conveyor belts. One boat can collect a maximum load of about 600 tons. The algae is unloaded at a processing plant that will extract the kelp's useful chemicals and send them off to be made into tasty treats —— many of which will end up on your dinner table. *Pass the seaweed, please!*

Longest Seaweed

Think forests only grow on land? When conditions are good, truly magnificent seaweed cities sprout from the ocean floor! A type of algae called Pacific giant kelp (*Macrocystis pyrifera*) forms the largest underwater "woods." Measuring up to 195 feet in length, this plant is the **Longest Seaweed** (pictured in the special color insert). It is also one of the fastest-growing plants, shooting upward as much as 18 inches in a single day. With this kind of speed, a handful of kelp seeds can explode into a watery wilderness in a few months' time. The thicket soon becomes an under- water apartment complex, providing shelter for thou- sands of ocean denizens.

Most Massive Plant

There are at least 47,000 suckers living right now in the Wasatch Mountains of Utah, USA — and we're not talking about easily fooled people. In December 1992, scientist Michael Grant discovered a 106-acre network of quaking aspens (*Populus tremuloides*) that looked like a forest, but which turned out to be the identical-twin shoots, or suckers, of one giant underground organism (pictured). Nicknamed "Pando" from the Latin for "I spread," this growth is estimated to weigh 6,600 tons, making it the **Most Massive Plant** on the planet. Most scientists think Pando is about 80,000 years old, but others claim it should have closer to a *million* candles on its cake. That's pretty impressive, especially when you consider that many people can't keep house-plants alive more than a few months.

Tallest Living Tree

The Stratosphere Giant, a coast redwood (*Sequoia sempervirens*), grows in the Rockefeller Forest of Humboldt Redwoods State Park in California, USA. Thrusting a magnificent 370 feet into the sky, the **Tallest Living Tree** should be easy to spot. Instead, trees that are almost as tall surround their record-holding neighbor (pictured). Scientist Chris Atkins managed to pick the Stratosphere Giant out of the crowd in August 2000, when a casual hike in the park brought him face-to-trunk with the terrific tree. "It was one of the most exciting moments of my life," says Chris, who used a laser-beam device to make his measurements.

A Stratospheric Secret

From the ground, it's hard to tell one tall tree from another, and this fact has made it possible for park rangers to keep the location of the Stratosphere Giant a secret from the public. They're taking this hush-hush approach to protect their prize plant, which they fear would be damaged by too much tourist traffic.

Tree lovers are disappointed but understand, given the fall of Tall Tree, another California redwood that once held the Guinness World Records title. In the 1970s, so many people traipsed around Tall Tree's trunk that the soil became hard-packed. The record-holder's root system became damaged. By 1990, the top 10 feet of the tree had died and crashed to the ground. Since then, the precise locations of the world's top trees have been kept under wraps.

Largest Seed

You might want to wear a hard hat when visiting the Seychelles islands in the Indian Ocean. This region is the home of the *coco de mer* or giant fan palm (*Lodoicea maldivica*), which bears a fruit containing the **Largest Seed** of any plant in the world (pictured). Its seeds start out the size of an acorn, hanging high up in the tree. Over the next 10 years or more, these seeds swell into 44-pound fruits the size of bowling balls. These ripe fruits create mini-impact craters when they fall off the tree. *Look out below!*

Longest Daisy Chain

Making daisy chains has been a childhood activity for centuries. Usually a single person strings together enough daisies to make a bracelet, a necklace, or perhaps a garland to wear on his or her head. But flower power ran amok on May 7, 1985, when 16 villagers from Good Easter, Chelmsford, Essex, UK, created the **Longest Daisy Chain**. The "chain gang" spent 7 hours making the blooming braid, which stretched an amazing 1.31 miles from end to end (pictured). That's long enough to create a circular garland about 2,200 feet in diameter. Good luck finding a person big enough to wear *that* colossal crown!

Chapter 4
Large Landmarks

Earth has many astonishing natural features. So why pick just a few out of the crowd? There has to be a truly ENORMOUS entry in every category — and Guinness World Records has collected information about each and every one of these fantastic formations! We'll stroll through our planet's craters, sand-surf its deserts, go rafting on its mighty rivers, and take an underground swim to its cavernous landmarks. Prepare yourself for an incredible journey of truly planetary proportions!

Largest Impact Crater

A 6-mile-wide asteroid or comet that hit Earth about 2 billion years ago made quite an impression, and our planet still has the scar to prove it (see illustration). The Vredefort Crater near Johannesburg, South Africa, has an estimated diameter of 186 miles, making it the **Largest Impact Crater** of about 150 known to scientists. Today, the outer parts of the crater are hard to see because most of it has eroded or has been covered with sediment. But an inner ring called the Vredefort Dome is still clearly visible. About 112 miles across, this configuration occurred when the Earth's crust bounced upward after the moment of impact. Great rebound!

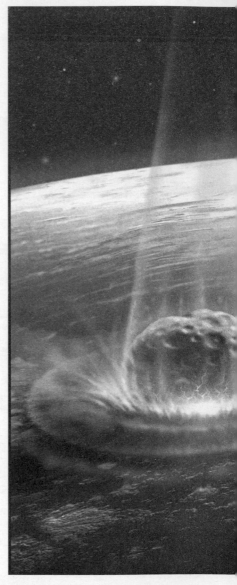

Simply Smashing

Earth has not experienced a devastating asteroid or comet impact for millions of years, but that doesn't mean it couldn't happen again. Our planet's impact risk is measured by the Torino Scale, which assigns danger ratings of 0 through 10 to all known space objects.

Rating Danger

0 No hazard (no chance of collision with Earth)

1 Normal (almost no chance of collision with Earth)

2-4 Merits attention (somewhat close encounters with a chance of striking Earth)

5-7 Threatening (close encounters that pose a serious threat to Earth)

8-10 Certain collisions (definite impacts, ranging from minor to catastrophic)

According to the US National Aeronautics and Space Administration (NASA), the scariest known space rock rates a "2." They'll be watching!

Longest River

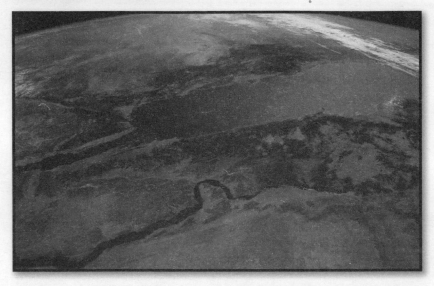

It's a strange but true fact that our planet's **Longest River** cuts right through the **Largest Desert** (see Record 18). The mighty Nile River of Africa begins in Burundi and travels through Rwanda, Tanzania, Sudan, and Egypt, including some bone-dry Sahara regions, before emptying into the Mediterranean Sea (pictured). From start to finish, the waterway is an astonishing 4,145 miles long — nearly twice the length of the Great Wall of China! At its mouth, the Nile discharges about 100,000 cubic feet of water per second. That's just a trickle compared to South America's Amazon River, which releases nearly 80 times that amount of liquid. But there's no denying that the weaker Nile goes the extra mile — and it earns a Guinness World Record along the way.

Largest Desert

You could fit all the preschoolers of the world into this super-size sand box. The Sahara Desert, which blankets most of northern Africa, is about 3,200 miles east to west, and between 800 and 1,400 miles north to south. The desert's total land area is about 3,579,000 square miles (that's nearly the size of all 50 American states combined), making this parched place the **Largest Desert** (pictured in the special color insert). Averaging about 3 inches of rainfall per year, it's also one of the driest regions anywhere. All that sand might remind you of the seashore, but don't be fooled. "Like, totally tubular, dude!" is one beach phrase you'll never hear in this sunny yet sea-free spot.

That ROCKS!

Travelers in some parts of the Sahara Desert can enjoy a little mountain music to help them on their way! When conditions are right, the sand dunes seem to "sing," blasting out noises that may sound like an orchestra, a drum section, or even the clash of military weapons. In the thirteenth century, explorer Marco Polo wrote that evil desert spirits caused these sandy songs. Modern scientists, however, feel that there might be something less mysterious at work. Researcher Bruno Andreotti from the University of Paris carried measuring equipment to the Sahara in 2004. He discovered that sand avalanches sometimes shake the faces of dunes, temporarily turning them into natural loudspeakers. He also found that the top volume of a singing dune was 105 decibels —— about equal to a snow blower or a fully cranked personal MP3 player. These findings bring a whole new meaning to the phrase "sand blasting"!

Longest Glacier

Get ready to chill out on one of the laziest rivers! The Lambert Glacier is a 40-mile-wide, 440-mile-long ribbon of ice that flows slowly through Australia's Antarctic Territory. Discovered by an aircraft crew in 1956-1957, this overgrown ice cube holds the Guinness World Record for the **Longest Glacier**. It's longer than the state of Florida! The rock-solid river drains about a fifth of the East Antarctic ice sheet and advances three-quarters of a mile per year toward the Amery Ice Shelf, where it empties into a spectacular slow-motion icefall (pictured). Meanwhile, back at the other end of the glacier, a new ice mass is just beginning the 400-year-plus journey. Zip up your coat, because it's going to be a long, cold ride.

Largest Cave

In January 1981, three men were exploring Lubang Nasib Bagus (*Good Luck Cave* in English) in Gunung Mulu National Park, Sarawak, Malaysia, when they discovered the **Largest Cave** in the world (pictured)! Also named the Sarawak Chamber, this colossal cavity is 2,300 feet long, 1,300 feet wide, and at least 230 feet high. To put those numbers into perspective, imagine an underground room filled with 747 jumbo jets parked in a 4x10 grid — about 40 of them! Three times larger than New Mexico's Carlsbad Cavern, the previous record-holder, the Sarawak Chamber is known today as one of Earth's most spectacular buried treasures.

Chapter 5
Monstrous Munchies

You don't have to bake, broil, or fry a thing to enjoy the heaping helpings of these record-setters. Get mushy over a car-size chocolate heart, exercise your creative flair with a couple of awesome food-based artworks, and help yourself to a slice of pizza. You can even nibble on a life-size gingerbread house taken straight from the pages of an old-fashioned storybook. Is all this food talk making you hungry? Let's cook up some super-size fun in the kitchen of Guinness World Records!

Largest Pizza

No matter how you slice it, this record-holder is one jaw-dropping pie! On December 8, 1990, the **Largest Pizza** ever created was baked at the Norwood Hypermarket in Johannesburg, South Africa (not pictured). Taking about 39 hours to prepare and bake, the monstrous munchie's ingredient list included 9,920 pounds of flour, 10,294 cups of water, 3,968 pounds of cheese, 1,984 pounds of chopped tomatoes, and 1,984 pounds of tomato puree. The finished pie was 122 feet 8 inches in diameter. It was topped with 1,763 pounds of mushrooms. Guess only one topping was permitted for this whopping order!

Great Pizza Performances

It might not have had the biggest surface area of any pizza. But for sheer length, a pizza created in Graz, Austria, definitely takes the cake . . . or, in this case, the pie. The Guinness World Record for Longest Pizza was set on June 1, 2006 (not pictured). Sami Ibrahim of Gasthaus Pizzeria zum Kerzenschein cooked up the cheesy champion measuring 591 feet 8 inches —— that's nearly the length of 3 football fields!

And while we're on the subject of pizza, let's take a moment to admire VF Corporation of Greensboro, North Carolina, USA, which ordered 13,386 pizzas for its 40,160 employees on August 19, 1998. That works out to be 1 pizza for every 3 people. The Largest Pizza Order was fulfilled by Little Caesar's, which delivered the piping-hot pies to 180 locations across the USA.

Largest Toast Mosaic

Some artists are moody, but Maurice Bennett of New Zealand is just plain crusty! Known as "The Toastman," Maurice is famous for creating larger-than-life mosaic portraits using thousands of bread slices singed to various shades of brown (Elvis portrait, pictured). His all-time **Largest Toast Mosaic** required 2,724 slices of bread (not pictured)! The final mosaic measured 39 feet 4 inches by 13 feet 5 inches. Displayed in Wellington, New Zealand, from February to March 1999, the enormous arrangement displayed the face of Mark Blumsky, the city's former mayor. Was it art or breakfast? Whatever you want to call it, raise a glass of orange juice in honor of this unique, record-setting creation.

Largest Jell-O Mosaic

Imperial College in London, UK, took a delicious trip when students used Jell-O bricks to build a Singaporean flag on the college's central lawn. Including 16,125 jiggly "tiles" and measuring 42 x 65 feet, the finished flag was not just patriotic; it was also the **Largest Jell-O Mosaic** ever created. About 200 students helped to build the edible artwork, which was put together on February 21, 2004. The record-breaking effort was organized by the college's Singapore Society, which dubbed the event "Flag-Gel-Lah" to recognize the three main aspects of the event: the flag, the gelatin, and the word "lah," which is often used by Singaporeans to add emphasis to sentences . . . LAH!

Stuck Together

Here are some artists' mosaic methods:

Direct method: Stick individual tiles —— or toast or Jell-O —— directly onto the final surface.

Double direct method: Stick tiles onto a larger piece of mesh, cut into smaller chunks then reassemble at the installation site. Good for large projects but has an uneven mosaic surface.

Indirect method: Smooth mosaic surfaces require sticky sheets. Press tiles facedown onto one sticky sheet, then peel and stick for small projects.

Double indirect method: For large projects, press tiles faceup onto a sticky sheet. Use a second sticky sheet to hold everything together. Peel away the first sheet and stick to the final surface.

Largest Individual Chocolate

It was a chocolate lover's dream . . . and a dieter's nightmare! In 2004, online dating organization Match.com teamed up with marketing consultant Marco de Comunicación to create a chocolate heart that was 16 feet wide and 13 feet high. Weighing in at 15,026 pounds, or about as much as four passenger-carrying cars, the tremendous treat was the **Largest Individual Chocolate** ever created (pictured). It was displayed at the Hard Rock Café in Madrid, Spain, from February 13 to 19 — just in time for Valentine's Day. Why was the super-size sweet created in the first place? "The record-breaking chocolate heart is really a celebration of dating, romance, and love," explained Trish McDermott, Match.com's Vice President of Romance.

Largest Gingerbread House

The phrase "Home Sweet Home" came to life in December 2001, when the **Largest Gingerbread House** ever built went on display at the Wolfchase Galleria in Memphis, Tennessee, USA (pictured in the special color insert). The scrumptious structure was 57.5 feet tall at its highest point and approximately 29.5 feet along each side, for a total internal volume of 33,196 square feet. Designed and built by Roger A. Pelcher, the house included 3,000 sheets of gingerbread weighing 4 pounds each, 4,600 pounds of icing "mortar," a 3,600-pound chocolate chimney, 500 pounds of assorted Christmas candy, and 250 pounds of peanut brittle. You'd never have to visit a candy store again if you lived in this delicious dwelling!

Mountains of Grounds

The Nestlé Corporation brewed up a headline-breaking publicity stunt on May 13, 2004, when it unveiled the Largest Cup of Coffee in New York City, New York, USA, at 8 A.M. sharp —— just in time to tantalize thousands of caffeine-craving commuters. The mighty mug was 5 feet 7 inches tall and 4 feet 8 inches wide, and it contained 660.5 gallons of latte. That's equal to 10,568 cups, which should be more than enough for even the most dedicated coffee lover. The ingredient list for the big beverage included 500 gallons of water, 45 pounds of instant coffee, and 475 pounds of vanilla-flavored Coffee-Mate Latte Creations powder, the product Nestlé was promoting with its super-grande-venti java junket.

Chapter 6
Colossal Collections

Have you ever meant to have a tiny taste, but ended up wanting more? That's kind of what happened to the people you'll read about in this section. Instead of food, these men and women found their treats in collecting ordinary objects, from buttons to rubber duckies. We'll marvel at the five colossal collections awarded with the ultimate prize: a Guinness World Record acknowledging these examples of astonishing dedication.

Largest Collection of Buttons

Back in 1983, Dalton Stevens of Bishopville, South Carolina, USA, had trouble sleeping. One sleepless night, Stevens became so bored that he got up and sewed a few buttons onto a shirt . . . and a nightly distraction became a dedicated hobby. Today, Dalton has collected 439,900 buttons with no duplicates, thereby breaking the Guinness World Record for the **Largest Collection of Buttons**. Appropriately known as the "Button King," he has decorated a full suit (164,333 buttons), a car (149,000 buttons), a guitar (3,005 buttons), and many other objects (pictured above, and in the special color insert). He has even decorated his own coffin (60,000 buttons), leaving room inside for a few important extras. "My last request is to be buried with a bag of buttons, a needle, thread, and a flashlight . . . just in case I wake up and have nothing else to do," Dalton says with a grin.

Largest Rubber Band Ball

He Had a Ball

John Bain's bosses probably weren't too happy when they heard about his particular quest for a Guinness World Record. While working in the company mailroom, John started collecting spare rubber bands and forming them into a ball. He picked away at his project for the next several years, eventually wrapping up a rubber orb that weighed 3,120 pounds when measured on October 22, 2003, at the Port Contractors in Wilmington, Delaware, USA. As the **Largest Rubber Band Ball**, this super sphere is 5 feet tall and 15.1 feet around, and it contains an estimated 850,000 rubber bands. Roll this mighty marble down a hill and watch it "lay some rubber" — for real! Bounce over to the special color insert to see John and his art project.

In creating a 1.56-ton rubber band ball, John Bain was snapped into reality when normal-size bands started to break. He wrote to Alliance Rubber of Hot Springs, Arkansas, explaining that he wanted to break the Guinness World Record, and needed their sturdier bands as stronger source material. The company sent John boxes of high-quality bands. For the next two years, he spent a couple of hours every day in his garage wrapping rubber, listening to loud music, and dodging any broken bands that catapulted outward from his record-breaking orb.

Largest Gnome and Pixie Collection

Ann Atkin of West Putford, North Devon, UK, was painting a landscape many years ago when a realization suddenly hit. *The landscapes need gnomes in them,* she thought. Ann got right to work bringing her vision to life, collecting every model gnome and pixie she could find. Today, Atkin has assembled 2,032 of these charming and fabled creatures into the **Largest Gnome and Pixie Collection**. She shares her world with the public on her 4-acre Gnome Reserve and Wild Flower Garden (pictured). Every year, about 25,000 people visit the reserve, where they are asked to don pointed gnome caps so they won't offend the local residents. "Take your cameras and embarrass the family," says Ann, who has a sense of humor about her fairy tale friends.

Largest Collection of Rubber Ducks

Every day is just duckie at Charlotte Lee's home in Santa Monica, California, USA. As the proud owner of the **Largest Collection of Rubber Ducks**, Charlotte is surrounded by the painted-on grins of 2,583 plastic pals as of April 3, 2006 (pictured in the special color insert). She has been collecting since 1996, starting with the purchase of a pack of three rubber duckies for her bathroom . . . and she kept on going. Today, Charlotte is outnumbered and that's the way she likes it. Surprisingly, she can't single out a favorite duck: "I love them all! They're all unique and wonderful in different ways," she explains. And who can blame her? No matter which way you turn your head, this cheerful collection is guaranteed to quack you up.

Quack Attack

Little duckies are big business in the hands of Great American Merchandise & Events (GAME), an organization that helps companies organize races for rubber duckies. GAME provides up to 20,000 numbered duckies and all the necessary paperwork. The organizing company then sells the duckies to the public for a few dollars apiece.

On race day, all of the duckies are dumped into a waterway, and before you can say "quack attack," the plastic tide starts to drift downstream toward a banner-bearing finish line. The fastest floaters win prizes for their owners. To date, duck races have raised more than $70 million, making this fun event a great fund-raiser.

Largest Set of Russian Nesting Dolls

It's ironic that a classic Russian art form has been used to celebrate American patriotism, but that's the case with the **Largest Set of Russian Nesting Dolls** (not pictured). Created by former Russian citizen Youlia Bereznitskaia, the set includes 51 hand-painted pieces that fit snugly inside each other. The biggest piece is the USA itself, standing 1 foot 9.25 inches tall, with an "America the Beautiful" theme. The other 50 pieces represent the 50 states and are progressively smaller, tapering down from Alaska to Rhode Island at the smallest, 0.12 inches. The record-breaking tribute started in St. Petersburg, Russia, on America's patriotic date of July 4, 1999, a few years before Youlia and her family emigrated to America. She finished her labor of love for her newly adopted country in Cameron, North Carolina, USA, on April 25, 2003. The entire process lasted about 46 months. Not bad for a collection that sums up 230 years of American history!

From Russia with Love

Russian nesting dolls are properly called *matryoshka*. This art form dates back to the year 1890, when a Russian artist named Sergei Maliutin became inspired by a set of Japanese nesting dolls. Sergei believed he could make his own version of the toy. Before long, nesting dolls became a phenomenon in the Russian art world. Today, *matryoshka* are so common in Russia that they are practically a symbol of the nation.

Early *matryoshka* showed Russian families, fairy tales, and traditional symbols. Today, you can commission one-of-a-kind designs or choose from these available themes:

- Politicians (including Russian leaders, American leaders)

- Celebrities (including The Beatles, Elvis Presley, Madonna)

- Cartoon characters (including Spider-Man, Pokemon)

- Professions (including musicians, lawyers, clowns)

- Holidays (including Santa Claus, presents, snowmen)

- Entire sports teams

- Pets of all types

Chapter 7
Built Big

"Construction Crews Gone Wild!" That would be a good title for a documentary featuring the five record-setting structures in this section, all of which are the most massive members of their respective families. Prepare to hang out on Hollywood movie sets, take a tour of NASA's home, and sit atop a sky-piercing spire. Can you feel the excitement building? Turn the page to experience some of humankind's most amazing architectural achievements!

Largest Indoor Film Set

Director Steven Spielberg is known for his global-themed, big-budget films with astonishing special effects. So it's not surprising that when the award-winning director needed a UFO landing site for the climax of his 1977 film, *Close Encounters of the Third Kind,* he ordered up the construction of the **Largest Indoor Film Set** in motion-picture history! Six times the size of the biggest Hollywood set, the staggering soundstage measured 90 x 450 x 250 feet, and was erected inside a 10-million-cubic-foot dirigible hangar in Mobile, Alabama, USA. The structure included about 4 miles of scaffolding, 16,900 square feet of fiberglass, and 29,500 square feet of nylon canopy — plus one larger-than-life, alien spaceship (pictured).

Largest Land-Based Prop

What's Up with the Horse?

Millions of people ponied up the admission fee to *Helen of Troy*, the 1956 movie that featured the **Largest Land-Based Prop** ever built (pictured in the special color insert). The eye-popping object was a 60-foot-long, 40-foot-high wooden horse that weighed 179,191 pounds, including 1,000 pounds of nails and a wagonload of screws, wooden pegs, and iron rings. It took the wood of 30 trees to build the enormous equine, whose hollow interior was air-conditioned for the comfort of the 25 actors who had to ride inside. *Hey, no horsing around in there!*

The big star in *Helen of Troy* came from Greek mythology. According to legend, Greek forces attacked the town of Troy in Asia Minor. A tall wall surrounded the town, and the Greek army couldn't find a way through the structure. They camped outside and awaited Troy's surrender. Ten years later when Troy still refused to surrender, the Greeks decided to try a new tactic. They built a humongous wooden horse, hid 40 men inside the hollow shell, and wheeled the "gift" up to Troy's front entrance. The Trojans thought the long siege was over, so they pulled the Greeks' strange present into the city. Later that night, when the Trojans were asleep, the Greek soldiers popped out of the horse and flung open Troy's gates. The rest of the army entered the city and conquered it, thereby winning the decade-long battle.

Longest Bridge

To local residents, it's just another way to get to work. But to the rest of the world, it's a record-setting marvel! Connecting the Louisiana towns of Mandeville and Metairie, the Lake Pontchartrain Causeway consists of two side-by-side roadways (pictured). The first roadway was built in 1956 and stretches 23.86 miles across the lake. The second roadway, added in 1969, is a tad more tremendous at 23.87 miles — a measurement that earns this span the title of **Longest Bridge**. Want to hit the road and cross this bridge when you get to it? Check your gas tank. There are no fuel stations along this arrow-straight avenue, and you don't want to run out of fuel halfway across this roadway.

Tallest Door

Rocket building rule #1: Make sure the rocket can fit through the door when you're done! Fortunately, architects didn't forget this important detail when they sketched out NASA's Vehicle Assembly Building at the Kennedy Space Center near Cape Canaveral, Florida, USA. Four 460-foot-high doors dominate the gigantic building, all of which share the Guinness World Record for **Tallest Door** (pictured). Each of these prodigious portals was designed to allow fully assembled Saturn and Apollo rockets to safely enter and exit the building entrance, minus any dangerous scraping. The Saturn and Apollo programs aren't active anymore, but Space Shuttles still shuffle in and out of these oversize openings.

Tallest Structure

If you stacked the Eiffel Tower, the Washington Monument, and Egypt's Great Pyramid, this gigantic superstructure still wouldn't surpass the KVLY-TV tower in North Dakota, USA (pictured). Jutting 2,063 feet into the sky, this television-transmitting mast holds the Guinness World Record as the **Tallest Structure**. Why so high? The low-population state of North Dakota doesn't have many broadcasting centers, so this single antenna serves a region larger than the District of Columbia, Hawaii, Massachusetts, New Jersey, and Connecticut combined. To cover that area, the transmitter has to be sky-high — and anchored to the ground by 40,125 feet of steel guy wires. Now there's a TV anchor everyone can appreciate!

BY EXPANDING THEIR IMAGINATIONS . . .

© Drew Gardner/Guinness World Records

IT'S A SNAP!

What propelled John Bain to make the Largest Rubber Band Ball? He became fascinated with making art out of bendable, twistable, or glueable office supplies. Shoot over to "Super-Size Stuff" and "Monstrous Munchies" for other artists' masterpieces.

AND FANCIFUL COLLECTIONS

© Peter Brooker/Rex USA

JUST DUCKIE
"Me and My Rubber Duckie" might be Charlotte Lee's favorite song, but she keeps most of her yellow-tailed tub pals in glass display cases throughout her home. Count the numerous items inventively stored by people in "Colossal Collections."

THESE SUPERSTARS

DISPLAYED DEXTERITY

© Harrod Blank www.artcaragency.com

BUTTONED UP

Dalton Stevens never has idle hands. When not making music, the "Button King of Bishopville" keeps busy with needle, thread, and buttons. See more of Dalton's work in "Colossal Collections" and learn how people transform hobbies into entertainment in "Crowd Pleasers."

DEVELOPED GIRTH

© Guinness World Records

© George F. Mobley/National Geographic Picture Collection

A YAWNING CHASM

We use our mouths for lots of activities: talking, smiling, and blowing bubble gum bubbles. **Piggy Bank** mouths are for depositing money while **hippopotamus** mouths are used in territorial displays. Measure the girth of the **Largest Piggy Bank** in "Super-Size Stuff," and balance the scales in "Weighty Wildlife" and "Prodigious People."

FROSTED FAIRY TALES

© The Commercial Appeal/Nikki Boertman

SWEET SATISFACTION
Hansel and Gretel would have had a hard time resisting a nibble off this gingerbread house, a record-setter in real life. Tie on your apron and follow the recipes used in "Monstrous Munchies."

TRANSPORTED TITANS

© Photo by Herbert Orth/
Time Life Pictures/Getty Images

© Sergo Edisherashvili/Reuters

ROLLING ALONG

Michelin Tires wasn't around during the Trojan War, or the ancient Greeks might have outfitted the Trojan horse with the company's easy-to-roll treads. Grab your hard hat for the construction tales of "Built Big," then take a spin in "Traveling in GRAND Style."

SERENADED TRAVELERS

© Bruno Perousse/age footstock

TUNEFUL DUNES

The desert can play tricks on the minds of travelers, especially if the traveler is low on water while crossing the seemingly endless Sahara Desert. Some report seeing an oasis where sand, not water, flows for miles. Others claim the dunes sing to them. Read about the science behind the songs in "Large Landmarks."

GREW
LARGER-THAN-LIFE

© Mark Conlin/Seapics.com

AQUATIC HARVEST

Crops flourish under different conditions, requiring farmers to use special equipment in harvesting their land. You would need scuba equipment and a boat to check on the Pacific Ocean's daily yield of seaweed. Dig into "Gigantic Greenery" for more hardy plant life.

. . . TO BE A GUINNESS
WORLD RECORD-HOLDER!

In-SPIRE-ing

More facts about the KVLY-TV tower:

• The tower was built in 33 working days by an 11-person crew.

• The tower and guy anchors take up 160 acres of space.

• It took 864,500 pounds of steel to build the tower.

• The tower includes a service elevator so workers don't have to climb all the way to the top when repairs are needed. The elevator is controlled by a single 7,870-foot cable.

• The antenna on top of the tower is 113 feet high and weighs 9,000 pounds.

• In a 70-mile-per-hour wind, the tip of the tower sways back and forth approximately 10 feet.

• It would take a baseball 24 seconds to fall from the top of the tower to the bottom.

• If a metal wrench was dropped from the top of the tower, it would be zipping along at 250 miles per hour by the time it hit the ground.

Chapter 8
Traveling in GRAND Style

These record-holders are ready to roll, and you're going to travel right along with them. In the next few pages, you will stand inside humungous tires, feel miniaturized alongside a mechanical behemoth, cut corners in a block-long limo, ride the rails in a mile-long train, and crush cars inside a monster truck. These movers and shakers are big, bold, and guaranteed to get you where you're going in memorable, oversize style!

Let the Good Times Roll

Big wheels are always turning in Allen Park, Michigan, USA. This is the home of the Largest Tire Replica. Built by Uniroyal, this 12-ton, 80-foot-tall bruiser was first used as a Ferris wheel at the 1964-1965 New York World's Fair. Originally, 24 passenger-carrying gondolas hung where the tire treads normally are. During the festival, the wheel carried an estimated 2 million people, including former First Lady Jacqueline Kennedy and her children.

The object was "re-tired" at the close of the fair and moved to its current location near the Detroit Metro Airport, where it received rubber treads and a brand-new identity as a tourist attraction. Today, the walloping wheel appears in countless travel guides and has been featured on maps, in artwork, and even on Christmas trees in the form of a mini-ornament.

Largest Tires

Now, this is what they mean by the term "high roller"! Standing 13 feet 1 inch high, and weighing more than 8,800 pounds each, the **Largest Tires** anywhere are built by Michelin to fit onto the **Biggest Dump Trucks**. Each whopping wheel costs $30,000! The hefty price tag doesn't stop people from snapping up these enormous rubber rings. In fact, there is a worldwide shortage of mammoth tires. Michelin is pumping out the products as quickly as possible, but it can take a whole day to build one Guinness World Record–worthy tire (pictured in the special color insert). "We can't make them fast enough," says Michelin executive Jim Micali.

Largest Land Vehicle

Got a mountain to move? Then you need the RB293 bucket-wheel excavator, a massive machine that can easily shift hills from one place to another (pictured). As the **Largest Land Vehicle**, this 31.3-million-pound mechanical monster is 722 feet long and 310 feet tall, and it can move 8.475 million cubic feet of dirt in a single day. It manages this feat with the help of 18 super-size buckets, each of which can dig up 1,743 gallons of material with a single swipe. It would take just 14 of these stupendous scoops to fill an average-size swimming pool! The RB293 won't fit into your backyard, so this vehicle is a true parking nightmare.

Longest Train

You would be waiting a *loooong* time if you got stuck at the crossing gate while this tremendous train rumbled past the station. The **Longest Train** ever assembled was 4.57 miles long, and consisted of 682 ore cars pushed by 8 diesel-electric locomotives (not pictured). Linked together by BHP Iron Ore of Australia, this champion choo-choo traveled 171 miles from the company's Newman and Yandi mines to Port Hedland, Western Australia, on June 21, 2001. It carried more than 90,000 tons of iron ore, which was eventually loaded onto enormous ships. We don't know what music the sailors on those ships listened to, but we suspect it might have been heavy metal.

Massive or Mini?

A model-train attraction in Germany has trounced the Longest Train record — in miniature, that is! On October 19, 2004, employees of the Miniatur Wunderland exhibit in Hamburg assembled and ran a 584-car model train that was 339.9 feet long. The tiny titan was built to HO-scale, which means that each part was exactly $\frac{1}{87}$th the size of its real-life twin. Multiplying 339.9 by 87 gets you 29,568 feet, or 5.6 miles —— more than a mile longer than the awesome Aussie vehicle that holds the full-size record. Unfortunately for this mini-machine, scale *does* count when you're going for a Guinness World Record, so the German attempt has to settle instead for the title of Longest Model Train (not pictured).

Longest Car

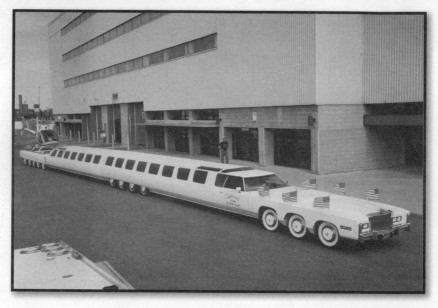

An entire high-school class could go to the prom in this lengthy limousine. Created by Jay Ohrberg of Burbank, California, USA, the **Longest Car** has 26 wheels and measures 100 feet from front fender to rear bumper (pictured). Those are some mighty measurements, especially for city driving. But tight turns are no problem for Jay's vast vehicle, which is hinged in the middle so it can bend around corners. Bottom line: This modified 1980 Cadillac will get you around town, but don't expect a cushy ride. Designed as a movie and advertising prop, the awesome automobile has no passenger seating. It does, however, feature a king-size waterbed and a swimming pool — diving board included.

Largest Monster Truck

When Bob Chandler of Hazelwood, Missouri, USA, built the first monster truck in 1975, he had no idea he was spawning a worldwide automotive obsession. People started copying Bob's super-size style, and before you could say, "Rev it up," everyone was claiming to have the biggest truck. So what did Bob do? He got the authorities in measurements to set the record straight, literally. The Guinness World Record for **Largest Monster Truck** belongs to Bigfoot 5 since 1986 (pictured). Weighing 38,000 pounds and standing 15 feet 6 inches high, this behemoth cruises through its occasional auto-show appearances on four 10-foot-tall Firestone Alaska Tundra tires. Part of a fleet of 17 Bigfoot trucks, the fabulous #5 is now on permanent display at Bob's company, Bigfoot® 4x4, Inc.

Chapter 9
Super-Size Stuff

What would inspire a person to build a piggy bank the size of a living room? Someone did, and you can read all about this and other objects of overwhelming size, including a towering teddy bear, a humungous bobblehead doll, and a cell phone perfect for a giant on the go. If bigger is better, then this super-size stuff is clearly the BEST — Guinness World Records–style!

Largest Cowboy Boots

The person clomping around in the **Largest Cowboy Boots** would wear shoe size 328-D, if such a person really existed. But the boots *are* real. The fantastic footwear is 3 feet 11 inches long, stands 4 feet 6.75 inches tall, and weighs 100 pounds (pictured). Go to El Paso, Texas, and pay a visit to Rocketbuster Boots. There you'll meet designer Nevena Christi and Marty Snortum, and their team of 15 cobblers — the people responsible for these record-setting soles. It took three months and $5,000 worth of materials, including nylon clothesline, to complete this custom-stitched creation by January 13, 1999. Today, the company employs 6 people and turns out 500 sets of regular-size footwear each year for such celebrity customers as Steven Spielberg, Meg Ryan, Arnold Schwarzenegger, and Oprah Winfrey.

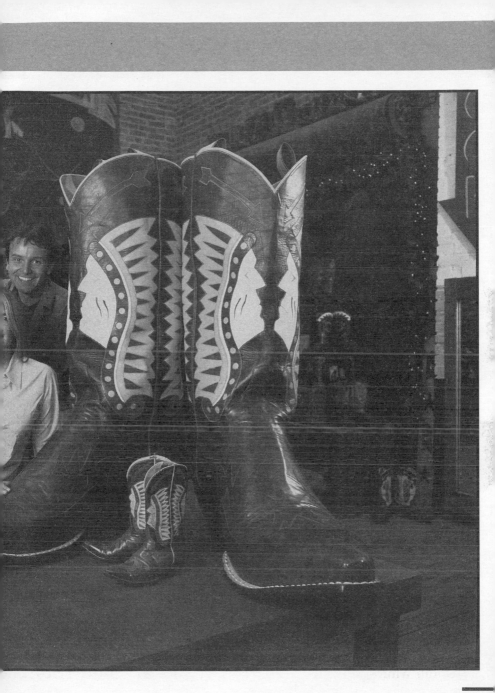

Largest Bobblehead

"When I began my career in show business, I never fathomed I'd have a bobblehead created in my likeness, let along the world's largest. It is one of the most bizarre tributes I could ever imagine," says U.S. game show host Chuck Woolery, the living model for the **Largest Bobblehead** ever built (pictured). The springy statue in question stands 11 feet high and weighs 900 pounds — and yes, its head really does *bobble*. Known as the "Chucklehead," the outlandish object was created by the Game Show Network and displayed at McCormick Place in Chicago, Illinois, USA, on June 8, 2003. It then took off on a national tour in the customized "Chuckwagon," traveling more than 3,000 miles by the time it completed its promotional duties.

Winning by a Head

The 2004 U.S. presidential election took place on Tuesday, November 2. But thanks to a few thousand bobbleheads, the St. Paul Saints minor-league baseball team knew the results several months in advance. On August 2, game attendees at seven sites owned by the Saints were asked to cast their vote for either George W. Bush or John Kerry, the leading presidential candidates. As a thank-you, each voter received a bobblehead doll of his or her chosen candidate. The bobblehead election turned out to be a nearly perfect mirror of the national election, matching the final results in six out of seven U.S. states. Does this experiment point the way to a whole new voting system? Maybe. "Our results were more accurate than exit polls. We didn't have three-hour waits or voting machine malfunctions. Plus, what would you rather have: an 'I voted!' sticker for the day or a bobblehead that's fun for the entire family?" said Jeff Goldklang, one of the event's organizers.

Largest Cell Phone

Cell phones seem to be shrinking as the years go by. But this record-holder reverses the trend in a really BIG way! The **Largest Cell Phone** ever built is called the Maxi Handy (Maxi Mobile), and it measures 6.72 x 2.72 x 1.47 feet. It was installed on June 7, 2004, at the Rotmain Center in Bayreuth, Germany, as part of a mobile communications exhibit (pictured). The mega-cool Maxi has a full-color screen and functional buttons, and it can send and receive real phone calls as well as SMS and MMS messages. The gadget is undeniably slick, but is it practical? Most of us believe that mobile phones should be, well, mobile — and no one could *ever* fit this device into their back pocket!

Largest Piggy Bank

You'd be rich if you had enough pennies to fill up the **Largest Piggy Bank** (pictured in the special color insert). Made in 2003 by Sampo Bank of Finland, this prodigious porker is 12 feet 6 inches tall, 17 feet 5 inches long, and 39 feet around. While the new record-holder hogs the spotlight, the previous record-holder did bring home the bacon in 2002. Pink Pig made a colossal contribution during its original mission as a promotional fundraiser for animal adoption in Frankfort, Kentucky, USA. The Davenport family (Chamberlain J., C. Michael, Little Bit, Kimberly, and Chandler T.) shows their personal appreciation to Pink Pig (pictured).

Largest Stitched Teddy Bear

Teddy bear lovers know that there are two types of stuffed bears: the ones with adjustable arms and legs, and the ones that are solid fluff and fur with no moving parts. Non-jointed teddies are also called stitched bears, and they can be much larger than their jointed cousins. Need proof? Consider the bearly believable example of Jody, a tubby teddy created by Dana Warren of Edmond, Oklahoma, USA (pictured). This fiber-filled critter measures 38 feet 8.2 inches from paws to ear tips, making him the **Largest Stitched Teddy Bear**. It took Dana six months to complete her creation, which was finished in 2001. Today, she runs a company called Bearly Yours that distributes mini-Jodies to needy children. Bear hugs all around!

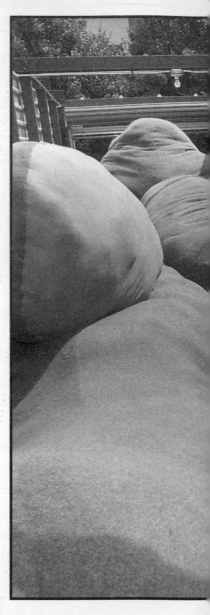

Teddy Trivia

You love your teddy, but do you really *know* your teddy? The fun trivia below will help you to become an expert on the bedtime bear. The hobby of teddy bear collecting is called arctophily. This is a combination of two Greek words meaning "bear" and "love." A school of fish, a pack of wolves . . . and a hug of teddy bears. Yep, that's the proper term for a group of these fuzzy friends. England, Germany, and the United States all claim to have created the first teddy bear. Most early teddy bears were made with real bear fur. Teddy bears are supposedly named after former U.S. president Theodore (Teddy) Roosevelt. In one famous story, Roosevelt refused to shoot a helpless bear on a hunting trip. The bear was dubbed "Teddy's Bear," and the nickname spread like wildfire. On the topics of wildfires, some firefighters and police officers carry teddy bears in their vehicles. They pull them out when they find a scared boy or girl who needs something soft and familiar to hug.

Chapter 10
Crowd Pleasers

Are you ready for some record-setting recreation? We'll play a people-size game of Monopoly, drive the loops of a gym-size Hot Wheels track, and hop a ride on a swing that's wider than a football field. There's even an entry for computer fans, itching to navigate a building-size video game. And we'll see a famous and gigantic statue vanish into thin air. Let the games begin!

Largest Permanent Monopoly Game

The real estate market is always booming in San Jose, California, USA, which is the home of the **Largest Permanent Monopoly Game** on Earth. Measuring 31 feet by 31 feet, the all-granite game was built by a company called Cypress Granite and Memorials as an exhibition for the 1992 San Francisco Landscape & Design Show. When the show was over, the city of San Jose bought the larger-than-life Parker Brothers classic and installed it in downtown Discovery Meadow (pictured). Opened to the public on July 26, 2002, Monopoly in the Park is now providing enormous entertainment to families, companies, school groups, and anyone else who feels like renting the big board for a few hours.

The Rules Still Apply

San Jose's giant Monopoly game is played by the same rules as regular Monopoly. But there are a few amusing twists that make mega-Monopoly an unforgettable experience for players and viewers alike. The houses, hotels, dice, and property cards are scaled to match the 961-square-foot board, so playing the game is a test of strength as well as strategy. The game is played by two-player teams. One team member wears a dog, an iron, or another classic Monopoly token on his or her head and acts as a living game piece. The other player runs to the bank, collects or pays rent, and performs other game-related errands. If you get sent to jail, you have to wear the black-and-white-striped prison uniform as long as you're in the slammer. Groups shell out $300 (that's real cash, not Monopoly money) to rent the board for three hours. The park provides the tokens, dice, houses, and other game gear, along with a banker, an announcer, and a game coordinator.

Longest Hot Wheels Track

Visualize the running track at your local school, then imagine a Hot Wheels speedway laid out around the outer edge — that's the size of the **Longest Hot Wheels Track** ever built! Measuring 1,650 feet in length and consisting of 2,100 pieces of track, the race-ready roadway would have been 20 miles long if it was scaled up to accept full-size cars. Mattel Canada, Inc. organized the project for Big Brothers Big Sisters of Canada and completed the track on July 7, 2002, at Thunder Alley in Toronto, Ontario, Canada. In 2006, another record attempt by Mattel, Inc. failed to connect when the sun warped the track (pictured).

Largest Game of Tetris

Engineering students at Delft University of Technology in Delft, Netherlands, put their video-game obsession on display when they built the **Largest Game of Tetris** ever devised in November 1995. To create the gigantic game board, the students installed lights in a grid of windows (15 stories high and 10 rooms wide) on the side of the 314 foot-tall Faculty of Electrical Engineering building (pictured). Forming a play-able area of about 21,500 square feet, the computer-controlled lights blinked on and off to represent falling blocks. Players used a regular-size joystick to rotate the blocks and drop them into place at the bottom of the "screen." Meanwhile, a crowd of observers gathered to watch the players' performances. Now, that's what we call a real block party!

Longest Swing

A bunch of lucky kids got into the swing of things at a village fete in Havelte, Netherlands, when they went for a ride on the **Longest Swing** ever built (pictured). It took 2 days for 8 volunteers to construct the astonishing playground staple, which included 132 wooden poles and 4,921 feet of rope. When finished on September 2, 1998, the seat of the stupendous swing measured 439 feet 7 inches from side to side. That's long enough to hold 288 children at the same time! Worried someone might fall off? The swing's builders made sure everyone would have fun and stay safe by adding safety jackets to their record-breaking ride. The only real problem, in fact, was putting the 6-ton seat into motion. One, two, three . . . Everyone pump your legs NOW!

Largest Illusion Ever Staged

Magician and illusionist David Copperfield (pictured) pulled history's biggest disappearing act in 1983, when he apparently made the Statue of Liberty vanish into thin air right before the eyes of an astonished live audience in New York City, New York, USA. This was no small feat. After all, the Statue of Liberty is 305 feet tall, and making it invisible was the **Largest Illusion Ever Staged**. The baffling trick was shown during a CBS television special called *The Magic of David Copperfield*. Was it just made-for-TV magic? People who witnessed the deed didn't think so. "If I was home watching it on TV I would be a little skeptical, but I was here, and [the statue] was there, and now it's not," said one impressed audience member. Jim Steinmeyer invented the trick, John Gaughan constructed the stage, and David Copperfield brought the magic — and none of these gentlemen will say how they did it!

Abracadabra!

Everyone wants to know how a magician pulls off those jaw-dropping illusions, but all professional illusionists make an oath never to reveal the science behind the magic to non-magicians. But their silence doesn't stop people from asking! The most believable theory about David Copperfield's record-setting illusion comes from author William Poundstone, who claims that magician and audience were positioned on a giant rotating turntable. When a silk curtain was raised, hiding the Statue of Liberty from the audience's view, the platform began turning slowly enough that the audience didn't notice the movement. David distracted everyone during this process with a lengthy speech about patriotism and all things American. When the platform had turned far enough, he wrapped up his speech, fluttered his magical fingers, and dropped the curtain. GASP! NO STATUE! Well, not exactly. The audience was now looking at the side of the statue. A tower at the front of the stage blocked Lady Liberty, who was waiting slightly offstage the entire time before making her grand reappearance.

BE A
Record-Breaker!

Message from the Keeper of the Records:
Record-breakers are the ultimate in one way
or another — the youngest, the oldest, the
tallest, the smallest. So how do you get to be a
record-breaker? Follow these important steps:

1. Before you attempt your record, check
with us to make sure your record is suitable
and safe. Get your parents' permission. Next,
contact one of our officials by using the record
application form at *www.guinnessworldrecords.com.*

2. Tell us about your idea. Give us as much
information as you can, including what the record is,
when you want to attempt it, where you'll be doing it,
and other relevant information.

    a) We will tell you if a record already exists,
    what safety guidelines you must follow during
    your attempt to break that record, and what
    evidence we need as proof that you completed
    your attempt.

b) If your idea is a brand-new record nobody has set yet, we need to make sure it meets our requirements. If it does, then we'll write official rules and safety guidelines specific to that record idea and make sure all attempts are made in the same way.

3. Whether it is a new or existing record, we will send you the guidelines for your selected record. Once you receive these, you can make your attempt at any time. You do not need a Guinness World Record official at your attempt. But you do need to gather evidence. Find out more about the kind of evidence we need to see by visiting our website.

4. Think you've already set or broken a record? Put all of your evidence as specified by the guidelines in an envelope and mail it to us at Guinness World Records.

5. Our officials will investigate your claim fully — a process that can take a few weeks, depending on the number of claims we've received and how complex your record is.

6. If you're successful, you will receive an official certificate that says you are now a Guinness World Record–holder!

Need more info? Check out *www.guinnessworld records.com* for lots more hints, tips, and some top record ideas. Good luck!

Photo Credits

The publisher would like to thank the following for their
kind permission to use their photographs in this book:

iv Grouse © Peggi Miller/iStockphoto; 5 (background) Mannequin © Belinda Gallagher/
Morguefile.com; 7 Sandy Allen © REX USA; 8 McCrary Twins © Bettmann/CORBIS; 10
Queen Marie Antoinette © Réunion des Musées Nationaux/Art Resource, NY; 11 Masang of
Padaung Tribe © Richard Vogel/AP Photo; 13 (background) Elephant, 21 (background) Daisies,
29 (background) Desert, 37 (background) Pizza, 45 (background) Buttons, 47 Rubber Bands,
53 (background) Bridge, 61 (background) Tire, 69 (background) Teddy Bear, 79 (background)
Swing © Morguefile.com; 14 Cane Toad © Michael Nichols/National Geographic Image
Collection; 16 Albatross © Jason Edwards/National Geographic Image Collection; 17 Thresher
Shark © Doug Perrine/Seapics.com; 19 Elephant Armor © The Board of Trustees of the
Armouries; 23 Pando © Jeff Mitton; 24 Northern Californian Giant Redwood Forest © Rex
USA; 26 Coco De Mer Seed © Wolfgang Kaehler/CORBIS; 27 Longest Daisy Chain Courtesy
of Good Easter Parrish Council, Essex; 30 Asteroid Impacts Earth Illustration © David A.
Hardy/Photo Researchers, Inc.; 32 Nile River Aerial View © NASA/CORBIS; 34 Beardmore
Glacier © Saul Pett/AP Photo; 35 Sarawak Chamber © Robert Dowling/CORBIS; 38 Pizza
Party © Fabrice Coffrini/AP Photo; 40 Maurice Bennett and Giant Toast Elvis Mosaic
© REUTERS/Neil Price MDB/DL; 42 Chocolate Heart, 66 Longest Limo, 70 Rocketbuster
Boots, 74 Maxi Mobile Phone © Guinness World Records; 46 Button King © Harrod Blank
www.artcaragency.com; 48 Gnome Reserve Courtesy of www.gnomereserve.co.uk;
50 Russian Nesting Dolls © James Benet/iStockphoto; 54 Close Encounters of the Third Kind
Courtesy of Everett Collection; 56 Lake Pontchartrain Causeway © Robert Holmes/CORBIS;
57 NASA's Vehicle Assembly Building © Kim Shiflett/NASA; 58 KVLY-TV Tower © Lynn
Trelstad; 63 Bucket Wheel Excavator SRs 8000 Courtesy of MAN TAKRAF Fördertechnik
GmbH; 64 Australian Coal Train © Claver Carroll/age footstock; 65 Model Train © Jane
M. Sawyer/Morguefile.com; 67 Bigfoot 5 © Neville Elder/Corbis Sygma; 72 Chucklehead
Courtesy of GSN; 75 The Davenport Family and Pink Pig Courtesy of Stephen M. Johnson/
Michael Davenport; 76 Dana Warren and Teddy © Jim Beckel/The Daily Oklahoman/AP
Photo; 80 Monopoly in the Park Courtesy of Orloff/Williams & Company; 82 Hot Wheels
Record Attempt © Fred Hunt/Hays Daily News/AP Photo; 83 Tetris Courtesy of the
Electrotechnische Vereeniging/TU Delft; 84 Largest Swing Courtesy of Het Volksfeest Havelte;
86 David Copperfield © Reuters.